NOT MY CHOICE BUT GOD'S

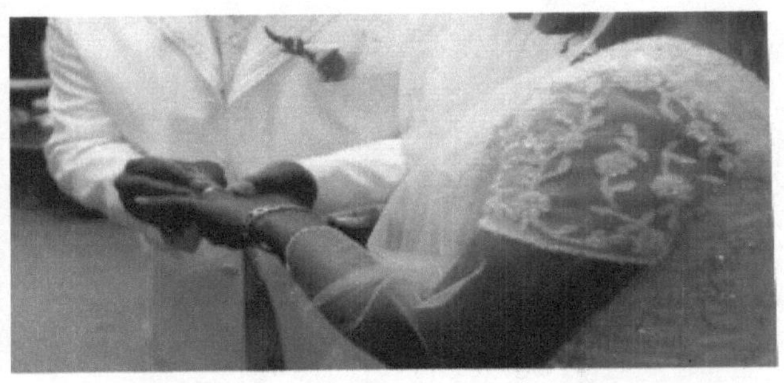

An approach to building a Kingdom Home based on divine pillars and foundations despite today's world of matrimonial confusion.

Nathan E-Olubiyi

Not My Choice But God's

Copyright © 2019

Table of Contents

ACKNOWLEDGEMENT

I give God the glory for His divine inspiration and credits must go to my Spiritual mentors – Daddy & Mummy Enoch Adejare Adeboye, Pastors Matthew and Yemisi Ashimolowo, Pastor and Pastor (Mrs.) Kayanja of Uganda, Rev. (Dr.) Ebenezer Ajitena and Pastor (Mrs.) Cecilia Ajitena for their moral and spiritual encouragements. Special credit to my spiritual leader Rev. (Dr.) E.O. Ajitena on his book (It is too late to fail) which encouraged me that "my determination to succeed will attract the divine attention of heaven" and that "the potency of my future and destiny is a direct result of exploiting my God-given potentials."

I belief 'now is my set time' to begin my contribution to the rebuilding of homes as a solid foundation for any successful society. Your teachings have spurred me into believing that I must develop a 'can do' attitude to all my live endeavours and this school of thought has led to the production of this book.

I also appreciate the fatherly support of Dr. Myles and Mummy Ruth Munroe for their continued Inspirational teachings; I also appreciate Mummy Toun Soetan in her wide knowledge of marital issues and the support of several anointed men of God whom I have come in contact with all through my marital choice wilderness experiences.
It also gives me a great pleasure to honour my beloved wife Izin and our children for their undiluted support and encouragement for my vision.

Nathan. E-Olubiyi

DEDICATION

This book is dedicated to the glory of the Lord Almighty who has saved me from the horrors of wrong marital trials over two decades; and has given me the grace to share my life experiences with others planning to choose their partners in this world of marital confusion; where a significant percentage of extremely wild and disobedient children are bred for our future.

Yes! Marital success is not by chance nor age,
- ➢ *It is not by technological acquisition,*
- ➢ *It is not by sound knowledge of family legal jurisprudence or education,*
- ➢ *It is not by your denomination nor religious belief,*
- ➢ *It is not by your wishes nor wealth,*

But By God's Will.

Only the genuinely broken can become a Master of Situation and circumstances – M.Sc. To be successful in marriage, you need to accept God's choice and break from who you used to, trust Him alone to lead you both in His will.

FOREWORD

The world as we see it today is full of matrimonial casualties. A global assessment of marital confusion and misdemeanour in our present day world is owing to that primordial act called "Decision Making". Seventy percent of marriages today are based on trial and error scheme, a substantial percentage of which ends up in Divorce. In my many years of counselling as a Pastor, I have noticed that the standard of marital life a couple would live depend absolutely on how good or bad their foundational decisions are.

How would you expect two self-haters to form a lovely marriage and build a happy home? It has often been said "If a man is not single, he must not marry"; What does it mean to be single, What makes you think you are maturely ready for the incredible journey called "marriage; Do you understand the structure of a Kingdom happy home? How would you weather various marital storms without capsizing your matrimonial vessel? This and many other interesting issues are crucial points the author has expatiated precept by precept in his prolific, articulate and scholastic style of writing.

I have personally seen this project as a masterpiece, well researched and an absolute necessity for ladies and gentlemen willing to build a role model happy family.

*In this Book " **Not my Choice; but Gods'"** the Author, Deacon Nat Olubiyi has expanded beyond reasonable doubt the possibility of experiencing matrimonial paradise in the present day world of overwhelming divorce. As you read along prayerfully, your heaven will open and you'll begin to concretize your marital foundation on the timeless truth throughout the pages of this Book. If you want to prevent poor performance in the future, prepare properly now. Marriage is a covenant and not a game of chance.*

Rev. (Dr) Ebenezer Ajitena.

Introduction

*Owing to past life and experiences in my great struggle
to have a home, the Holy Spirit challenged me to write
this book to encourage Singles and young ones of our 'jet
age' on how they can identify and enjoy divine approval
of God in making their marital choices in conformity
with Kingdom Doctrines.*

*The world of today is extremely perverse and so many
homes are broken because their foundations were not on
the everlasting Rock of Ages. The word of God says 'if
the foundation be destroyed, what can the righteous do'?
What about external influences as families, society,
'friends and fiends', the arrival of divinely ordained
inclusions and sojourners - children (who will come and
leave you and your spouse at majority age) into the family –
"And God blessed them, and God said unto them; be
fruitful, multiply………"Gen. 1:28*

*NOTE: It is true that no one is perfect, (as you may be
thinking right now), [sister/brother] but you can aspire*

to be a success in your own little Godly empire of your home, if you have Jesus Christ living in you and you plan to have Him as the Supreme Head of your home, with the potential husband as the chief administrative strategist of your home who deserves obeisance and total submission in compliance with the scriptures; with the potential mother in the home being the chief tactician in implementation of strategies mutually established in love.

This book I belief, will further encourage all singles to consider a serious study of scriptures - respect the sanctity of the institution of Marriage as a divine one and develop sound domestic communication skills to avoid or reduce conflicts as much as possible, before taking the plunge into marital life.

Remember – ("so shall a man leave his father and mother and cling unto his wife and they shall become one.....") before saying "I DO" at alter; BE PREPARED!

Reader, personal experiences I will share in the following pages will help someone out there to succeed in making Godly choices which will form the bedrock of building a solid foundation for their own successful homes. Our societies, communities and Nations of today are what they are, because our homes have failed in all God ordained responsibilities as the divine nucleus of the larger communities.

The height of moral decadence, pride and nonchalance often displayed by a significant percentage of today's youth is a direct reflection of homes where they were nurtured. The bible says teach your child in the way of the Lord; when he/she becomes of age, they will not depart from it. Unfortunately, scripturally untutored parents cannot give what they don't have. They would only depend on academic knowledge, societal influence or mere transfer of ignorance in bringing up their offspring.

MARRIAGE INSTITUTION IS NOT A CREATION OF MAN OR TECHNOLOGY *(That is, why what obtains as solution in Mr. "A's" home may not be the panacea for Mr. "B's" domestic situation. God's ways are beyond human understanding, so will His interests and manufacturer's manual for our individual lives differ at every given time.* ***SEEK GOD FIRST AND LET HIM OPEN YOUR INNER EYES OF DIVINE UNDERSTANDING BEFORE MARRIAGE TO AVERT FUTURE REGRETS.***

Chapter 1

WHAT IS DOCTRINE?

DOCTRINE arises from individual perceptions of principles of life, theories, postulations, schools of thought and other societal norms which consciously or unconsciously become a way of life or belief.

Kevin J. Conner says it means "something taught, teachings, instruction; the principles of religion that are taught; or more literally, 'to teach the substance'.

In context therefore, he says the term doctrine is used to refer to the truths of God's Word that are to be taught. For scriptural understanding, please refer to *Luke 1:1-4*

DOCTRINE AND ITS NATURE

> *It must be obeyed,*
> *It must be sound and scriptural,*

> *It must be pure and be able to determine the characters of its believers and affect fellowship, [Job. 11:4]*
> *It must be premised on Christ-like love,*
> *It must be Kingdom focused,*
> *It must be applicable without prejudice or favouritism,*
> *It must be premised on divine visions and not personal goals.*

For scriptural understanding please refer to [1 Tim. 1:3, 10, 4:16, 6:3] [2 Tim. 4:3, Titus 1:9, Titus 2:1, and 1 Pet.2:2]

SOCIETAL DOCTRINES

These arise from perceptions, opinions, thoughts of respected authorities in their fields, governmental regulations, local laws, precedents, imposed assumptions, etc. Different societies of the world have their individual norms which easily transform into doctrines either by application of enforcement powers or by divine order.

Doctrines could be premised on:

1.   *Religion*
2.   *Scientific Analysis and results*
3.   *Culture and Societal believes*
4.   *Events*

5.   *Individual Perceptions and positions*
6.   *Kingdom Principles*

In the foregoing, I will dwell more on Christian doctrines, its interpretations and what singles need to know in their individual plans for living a Christ-like life when they eventually wish to have a good life in Holy Matrimony.

HUMAN DOCTRINES

Mark 7:7-13 says the doctrines and traditions of men make the Word of God of no effect.

A further insight into the book of *Ephesians 4:14 gives credence to Paul's teaching that a Christian single should not be carried away by "spiritual gymnastics," etc.* There exists:

- The Doctrine of Balaam – *Rev. 2:4; II Pet. 2:15*
- The Doctrine of Jezebel – *Rev. 2:20-24*
- The Doctrine of the Nicolaitans – *Rev. 2:6, 15.*
- The Doctrine of the Pharisees and Sadducees – *Matt. 16:12; Luke 12:1; Acts 23:8.*
- The Doctrine of the Devil – Here Apostle Paul emphasized on happenings in the later times when men shall depart from the faith, giving heed to seducing spirits, pride and other doctrines of the devil just as we witness these days.

For further study please refer to Ephe.4:14, Gal. 1:6-8, Deut. 4:2, Prov.30:6, II Pet. 3:14-16, Exod.23:6

SPIRITUAL DOCTRINES COMPARED

CHRISTIAN DOCTRINE
- *Doctrine of God*
- *Doctrine of truth and peace*
- *Doctrine of prayer*
- *Doctrine of light*
- *Doctrine of Hope and meaningful life*
- *Doctrine of Life and freedom through Christ*
- *Doctrine of Christ and the Lord's kingdom*

DEVIL'S DOCTRINE
- *Regrets and failure*
- *Pride and self*
- *Satanic Assumptions and worldly theories*
- *Darkness and confusion*
- *Man's thoughts*
- *Deceit and Ruin*
- *Early death and bondage*
- *Duplication/Fake*

- *Uncreative but searches for weaknesses/faults*

SOUND DOCTRINE MAKES A CHRISTIAN SINGLE LIVE LIKE:

- A tree planted by the river side which brings forth its fruit in its due season. *(Psalm 1:3)*
- A refreshing image fully restored after severe storm, wilderness experiences, draught or famine. He receives the Word as they come and allows them to accomplish the purposes for which they have been sent by God. Please refer to *Heb. 6:4-9* for further understanding.
- A spiritual being, which daily loads himself with the word of God and accomplishes divine blessings and benefits. It is like yeast in the lump of flour. Please refer to *Ephesians. 1:3, Jude 3* for further study.
- A Kingdom watchman willing to rightfully share the words of knowledge and kingdom mandate to the understanding of others.
- Joseph was in abundance in the days of famine and lack,

- Solomon richly blessed with divine wisdom and wealth so much that he became a blessing to the world of his days,
- An epitome of righteousness, peace and joy in the Holy Ghost.
- A person who is encamped with the fire of the Holy Ghost because he/she has both divinely appointed security personnel – **goodness and mercy** *(unknown to the ordinary man).*
- A person to be envied by myopic minds who will always recount his/her past to judge his/her present.
- A person prepared and designed for heavenly glory that cannot be altered by men.
- A person whose achievements will confound the wisdom of the so called worldly wise-men who would always claim – "I know him/her very well. Is he/she not the son/daughter of this and that? Is he/she not my childhood pal? Is he/she not my brother/sister? Is he/she not my former ward, dependant? Is he/she not my former student?"

All these stories must be told of anyone whom God has blessed and is at the right place at the right time as Ruth in Boaz's field in ***Ruth Chapter 2.***

Patriarchs as Esther, Joseph, Hannah, Daniel and many others in the bible personified God's promises for those who diligently seek Him.

WHO IS A CHRISTIAN?

A Christian is an adherent of Christianity, member of a Christian denomination, especially by baptism, or a commendably decent or Christ-like person, *The Penguin English Dictionary.*

Ezek. 33 has epitomised the role of Christians as Watchmen. *"How can one reconcile the watchman of today being the real thief and evil minded representative of the devil?"*

For scriptural understanding, Please refer to Phil. 3:3, I Cor.2:6, I Cor.12:4

Worshippers of God were first called Christians in Antioch as the disciples led them in the doctrine of Christ for months and they were equally Christ-like in their ways– *Acts 11:26*

CHARACTERISTICS OF TRUE CHRISTIANS

- True Christians are sound in the knowledge of the Word and the life of Christ,
- Prayerful, watchful, bold and have faith in God,
- Applies themselves to sound doctrines of God, His Kingdom and proclamation of His kingdom principles for a purposeful life,
- Often aspire to be pure, loving, holy and have self control,
- Fears God and believe He can do all things,
- Always nursing the ambition of fulfilling God's purpose on earth,
- Hears from God through dreams, vision, etc. - *Job 33:15-16*
- Displays the knowledge of discernment of spirits – *Amos 3:7,*
- Available for God's work of evangelism/soul winning anytime,
- Worthy of emulation, as an evidence of accepting Christ as Lord and Saviour – *'behold old things have passed away and all things are become new'*
- Radically jealous for God and things of the Spirit,

- Always willing to claim the kingdom of God on earth violently in the spirit,
- Understands sound management of time – *Ecle. 3*
- Never allows assumptions or hear-say; but seeks to find out the real issues and establishes the truth,
- Does not indulge in excessive and reckless eating habit, but develops sound fasting and praying lifestyle to the glory of God. *Stomach for food and food for stomach; both will be destroyed by God one day.*

Why Reiterate Christian doctrine?

Christian doctrine should of necessity be reiterated, especially in these last days; as civilization, technology, greed, perverseness, and self-promoters have afflicted the church with so many vices that the church of today have lost its ancient tastes and salt as in the days of Moses, Elijah, Samuel, Peter, Apostle Paul, etc. The world now reigns in the church – worldly apparels, music, doctrines, etc.

Servants of the devil in cassocks and collars have imparted their sweet vibes, tales of confusion and self aggrandisement provoked by evil desires on the 'feeble minded and milk-fed' members.

Worldly Schools of Thought on Christian Doctrine

- 'God can't be real and he would allow things happen just like that' - Late Dr. Tai Solarin *(Nigerian)* on the death of his close friend,

- There are no biblical records of Christ or any of His Disciples formulating or giving any ready-made system of doctrine; but such schools of thought will never remind the milk-fed (Christian babes) of 'the Beatitudes' as in *Matt. 5:1-16,*

- Exhibition of excessive and meritorious righteousness even in context of biblical notes that no man on earth is righteous – *Ezek. 33:12-13, Luke 17:10,*

- Doctrines promotes divisive tendencies, leading to multi-denominations as we see today; forgetting the biblical prophesies in *Acts 2:17; II Tim. 3:1; II Pet. 3:3*

- Doctrine is dull, dry and useless for today's man (jet age or so called civilised man); forgetting that the Ancient of days and His doctrines never grow old. Usually such positions are premised on an individual's assessment of the material presenter. *Read II Tim. 3:10*

THE DOCTRINE OF GOD

God's doctrines are expounded in the teachings of Jesus Christ *[Mark 4:2);* and He said His Father and Himself are one in Doctrine *[John 7:16-17].*

The Message Bible says in **Romans 2:17** *[Religion Can't Save You] If you're brought up Jewish, don't assume that you can lean back in the arms of your religion and take it easy, feeling smug because you're an insider to God's revelation, a connoisseur of the best things of God, informed on the latest doctrines! I have a special word of caution for you who are sure that you have it all together to yourselves and, because you know God's revealed Word inside and out, feel qualified to guide others through their blind alleys and dark nights and confused emotions to God. While you are guiding others, who is going to guide you? I'm quite serious. While preaching "Don't steal!" are you going to rob people blind? Who would suspect you? Same with adultery and idolatry. You can get by with almost anything if you front it with eloquent talk about God and His law. The line from Scripture, "It's because of you Jews that the outsiders are down on God," shows it's an old problem that isn't going away.*

I say, many elites are down on God and the scriptures because of today's Christians. Gullible and unlettered people can be easily tossed around with eloquence and knowledge of cultures, but not those who Christ said of that, **'they will not believe until they have seen signs and wonders'.** That was corroborated in a real life situation where a qualified Medical practitioner witnessed the miracle of God in a case of a terminally ill patient of his in London and said *"Honestly!!! It is a mystery"*. Many more of such will convert such professional pundits without doubt. A Christian single should get to a level of spiritually decreeing a thing to be a worthy representative of God in marriage.

The truth is, how many Christian of today can boldly confront common stress induced headache in the family with the blood of Jesus Christ? Our God is not deaf to our calls, but our iniquities have taken us far away from His   presence.
For further study Please refer to ***Titus 2:1, I Tim. 6:1,3; Isa.29:24; Deut. 32:2, Prov. 4:2, 1*** st ***John 1:9*** from the same version of the Holy Bible.

Chapter 2

WHO IS A SINGLE PERSON?

A single person is an unattached or unmarried male or female individual, a unique biological being created in the image of God for a divine purpose on earth.
Nathan Olubiyi

A single Christian person combines the nature of Christ as explained in the definition of Christians with maturity in preparation for a blissful, peaceful, harmonious and prosperous matrimony.

He/She is expected to have passed through certain levels of tutelage through direct parental nurturing and care, relations, friends, neighbours, institution of learning, religious institutions, peer group, societal norms, governmental regulations and decrees, etc.

He/She would have acquired some skills contingent to the thought of independence and eventually seeking *'private and confidential'* companionship. Such skills when acquired, prepares us all for 'our tomorrow, our homes, our children, our community and our nations'.

He/She would have reasonably climbed and fulfilled the Maslow's hierarchy of needs before considering the need for a choice confidant. He/She would have attained majority both physically, emotionally and mentally. *Christian Marriage is not for children – boys and girls.*

Maslow's Hierarchy of Needs: Maslow *(1954)* presents a hierarchy of needs pyramid which can be divided into basic needs (e.g. physiological, safety, love, and esteem) and growth needs (cognitive, aesthetics and self-actualization).

One must satisfy lower level basic needs before progressing on to meet higher level growth needs. Once these needs have been reasonably satisfied, one may be able to reach the highest level called self-actualization.

"Every person is divinely designed to be capable and have the desire to move up the hierarchy toward a level of self-actualization". Unfortunately, progress is often disrupted by failure to meet lower level needs either by externalities of life or personal ignorance and laziness. Life experiences including divorce and loss of job may cause an individual to fluctuate between levels of the hierarchy. Maslow noted only one in a hundred people become fully self-actualized because our society rewards motivation primarily based on esteem, love and other social needs - *www.simplypsychology.org*.

These hierarchies of needs include:

1.   Biological and Physiological needs - air, food, drink, shelter, warmth, sex, sleep, etc.
2.   Safety needs - protection from elements, security, order, law, limits, stability, etc.

3.   Belongingness and Love needs - work group, family, affection, relationships, etc.

4.   Esteem needs - self-esteem, achievement, mastery, independence, status, dominance, prestige, managerial responsibility, etc.

5.   Self-Actualization needs - realizing personal potential, self-fulfilment, seeking personal growth and peak experiences.

THE Scriptures

Genesis 2:24 Therefore a man shall leave his father and his mother and shall become united and cleave to his wife, and they shall become one flesh.

Matthew 19:5 And said, For this reason a man shall leave his father and mother and shall be united firmly (joined inseparably) to his wife, and the two shall become one flesh?

Mark 10:7 For this reason a man shall leave [behind] his father and his mother and be joined to his wife and cleave closely to her permanently,

Ephesians 5:31 For this reason a man shall leave his father and his mother and shall be joined to his wife, and the two shall become one flesh.

While not castigating those who choose to co-habit in same sex relationships; (relying on God's mercies and their earthly liberties backed up by earthly laws); we are concerned specifically here about those genuine Christians who committedly adhere to scriptural injunctions and are desirous at harkening to the voice of God and His Word, in Godly marriage between male and female as created by God, with the hope of glory in Christ Jesus at the end of their lives.

Moses said in **Deuteronomy 30:19** *I call heaven and earth to witness this day against you that I have set before you life and death, the blessings and the curses; therefore choose life; that you and your descendants may live.*

King Solomon said in **Proverbs 11:19** *He who is steadfast in righteousness (uprightness and right standing with God) attains to life, but he who pursues evil does it to his own death.*

Prophet Jeremiah said in **Chapter 8:3** *of his book that "And death shall be chosen rather than life by all the residue of those who remain of this evil family (nation), who remain in all the places to which I have driven them, says the Lord of hosts."*

He or she would have developed Godly personalities relevant to the fulfilment of life purposes as replenishing the earth through your personal contributions, subdue it by identifying your hook, your target fish by developing yourself in anyway relevant to your vision, have dominion on the animals and fishes and every other non living things, thereby having influence on others through your peculiar skills, talents and potentials. This is when strangers shall begin to submit themselves to you and people who have not known you shall begin to obey your instructions.

Bill Gate today, through his Microsoft prowess and world acclaimed software institution and ministry even commands Presidents, Prime Ministers, Kings and subjects through the commands his company engineers have written into all Office and Home Windows operating systems and application packages. If you hate Bill Gate, you cannot hate his product that gives you convenience and efficiency. The bible says, *when your ways please God, He'll make your enemies to be at peace with you.* Please note that I am not saying "my friend Bill" is a saint.

With all these preambles, please prepare your mind as you read on. Check yourself if you are in a Godly marital relationship or indeed prepared for a *'private and confidential'* Christian marital relationship as a Bachelor or a Spinster.

Chapter 3

BASIC FOUNDATIONAL ISSUES OF LIFE A CHRISTIAN SINGLES NEED TO CONSIDER BEFORE STARTING A HOME

- Is my belief and faith in Christ unshaken?
- Have I truly repented from my dead works?
- Having accepted Christ, am I now truly a new creature?
- Have I been baptised by the Holy Spirit not just by immersion?
- What are my thoughts of eternal judgement (if suddenly my trumpet from the Kingdom sounds now?
- What is my perception of a Christian Home?
- Can I differentiate between permissive will and the perfect will of God?
- What are my considerations for a life partner who would not jeopardise my eternal life for the earthly home in the type of marital love we hope to build?
- Who truly is my spiritual mentor or role model, because the bible says iron sharpeneth iron?

- Will friends, family or financial considerations influence my choice of a Godly life partner?

- Can I design and influence a *'Trust norm'* in my home? This implies both partners preparing to trust one another, be trust worthy and be willing to create a trust building relationship by telling the truth behind your actions to your spouse?

- Are you willing to do away with your parlance of "I am going somewhere", "I am doing something", "I will check if I have some funds in my account", etc.

- Can you share your account secrets with your spouse? If he/she shares such information with you, will you be mature and sensible enough to have a mutual understanding always, without unnecessary demands?

- Will physical or mortal considerations be my basis for choosing my partner?

- Am I mature enough and willing to say I do again after 10 years in marriage, whatever the prevailing situation?

- Can God count on me in keeping to my marital vows?

ARE YOU A LIGHT IN YOUR ENVIRONMENT?

***Oxford advanced learner's dictionary** writes that **light** makes it possible to see things;*
***Light** brings to knowledge some information that were hitherto unknown to people;*
***Light** brings an end to darkness;*
***Light** moves known to the unknown. That is, light illuminates, expounds and reveals things you thought you have known to you in a new understanding,*

*Scripturally, **light** Reveals – John 14:16*
***Light** Guides – John 12:46*
***Light** exposes chaos – Phil. 2:15*
***Light** discriminates between Godly and ungodly living – John 8:12*
***Light** illuminates – Ephe. 5:8-9*
***Light** penetrates – 1ˢᵗ Thess. 5:5*
***Light** enlightens – John 12:35*
***Light** warns of danger – Ephe. 5:11-14*
***Light** protects Rom. 13:12*

With the understanding of what light is, you will need to appreciate the fact that your involvement in matrimony will expose you to another level of worldly activities, personalities, environments, schools of thought, financial pressures, a renewed need structure, etc.

The bible says… **we are the light of the world. No one lights a lamp and puts it under a bushel. Your matrimony should be** an embodiment of success, blissful love, care, affection, humility, and a relationship worthy of emulation even if by one or two persons/neighbours. ***Never, expect another couple's light to provide 100% light to your family situation.*** You can only pick those areas you feel will benefit your home and let them receive illumination from your near perfect setting as well.

Be a light to your own home – wife, husband, children, dependants, extended family members, friends, and other associates. The bible says let your light shine so much that people of the world will see and give glory to your Father in heaven.

To be a light, ***your lifestyle must preach the gospel of the Kingdom*** wherever you find yourself. Note that you will surely have objections, envy and deliberate resentment owing to your Kingdom believes.

Strive, to ***show yourself approved to those who understand God's principles and injunctions*** and not to the Charlatans who dwell richly in abominations as in 'Nations where Satan lives'.

The bible says *'let the words of my mouth and the meditation of my heart be acceptable unto you oh! Lord'*. Yes, as a light of the world, careless talk and association should be abhorred as much as possible.

Identify the real persons behind those you consider to be your friends, check them out in their use of words, lifestyle and company. Are they reckless in the use of words especially to honourable men of God?

As there abound dis-honourable men of God who practice the deeds of those serving the devil in 'countries where Satan lives'.
Rev. 2:13 I know where you live—a place where Satan sits enthroned. [Yet] you are clinging to and holding fast My name, and you did not deny My faith, even in the days of Antipas, My witness, My faithful one, who was killed (martyred) in your midst—where Satan dwells.

Truly, many highly positioned 'Ministers of God' in the Christendom of today still indulge in abominable practices; however, please register it in your mind that some are still exemplary in their daily conducts and God is proud of them any-day.

Psalm 145:14 *The Lord upholds all those [of His own] who are falling and raises up all those who are bowed down.*

Isaiah 28:7-8 *These also, the priest and prophet, stagger from drink, weaving, falling-down drunks, Besotted with wine and whiskey, can't see straight, can't talk sense. Every table is covered with vomit. They live in vomit.* The Message Version of the Holy bible.

Satan is synonymous with works of darkness and the children of light will never be found associating with children of darkness. If your friend is toying with darkness, help him/her in form of advice, if he/she insists, pray, and if no repentance flee as much as you can. He/she is obviously and divinely doomed for perdition.

MONEY

Yes, a mere creation of man as a means of economic exchange. *Never look out for financial gains in your relationship.* Let God bless you and your spouse with His heavenly blessings with the best promise of adding no sorrows with it.

Jesus Christ in His days of physical sojourn on earth did not belief in money, but to satisfy the 'earthly powers of His age' only offered to give what is Caesars' to Caesar and He instructed Peter to pick coins from the mouth of a fish in the river and give it to those who want to live by money.

Just have it in mind that blessings from God surpass money; it is wholesome and comes with – good health, peace of mind and obedient children, happy home, love of Godly issues and divine elevation.

Your blessing from God has nothing to do with your personal achievements, fame, acquaintances, family background and other myopic considerations. ***The Lord said, I will bless whoever I wish to bless.*** All you need do is to put your total trust in Him; love what He loves, hate what He hates - simple!! Many have earthly money but lack peace of mind, no joy, but have happiness in their human achievements; they have money but still nurse deep sorrows when they see those who are not as rich in earthly things as themselves being divinely blessed of God.

Physical Appearance/Good Health

Yes, the world of today will consider these before God's wishes for them. ***I must say here that our God will always want to use any available 'tool' to glorify Himself.*** If you have genuinely sought His face prior to making your choice, He will not give you any temptation that will overwhelm you. He will always make a way of escape, even if you are almost falling.

If God has spiritually established/confirmed to you both that you are meant for one another, accept that he/she is yours and move on (believing that God wants to glorify Himself in your situation). The three Hebrew young men asserted that even if God fails them, yet they will not bow down to any other god or image and God did not fail them. The king himself saw a fourth person in the burning furnace - *'an image that looked like the image of the Son of God'*. See *Dan. 3:24-25*

Prepare your mind for the representative of God Almighty- the *Holy Spirit* (Godly 3rd person) in your proposed home to lead, guide and chastise you to make your ways straight and give you everlasting joy in your matrimony.
For further studies, pls. read Proverb 5, 10 and 11.

LOVE: GOD IS LOVE

Paul *the Apostle of Christ* said *(and in my own words)* that, even if we can sing as Nightingale, speak queen's English as the Queen of England herself, be another Bill Gate, build up fame like David Beckham and other Holy wood stars; we are nothing without love. Our Lord Jesus Christ epitomised love by volunteering Himself to put on man's image in order to pay the supreme price of shame and death for our sins and transgressions.

- **Love your country -** *Psalm 137, Judges 5:1-31*

- **Love your neighbour as yourself** – *Job 42:11, Luke 7:2-6, John 11:16, Mark 5:18*

- **Love your Church** – *Psalm 122:6, 9, Isaiah 22:4*

- **Love yourself by studying and meditating on the Word daily –** *Deut. 4:10, Deut. 13:3, Deut. 29:29, Deut. 17:19, Josh. 1:8.*

- **Honour your parents and everyone who is older than you, so that you may live long and enjoy the covenant of God –** *Gen. 26:23, Gen. 6:18, Gen. 17:7 Exod. 20;12, Mal. 1:6.*

- **Love the Lord's revelation -** *Amos 3:7*

Chapter 4

CHOOSING A LIFE PARTNER

Understanding **"SENSITIVITY AND INSENSITIVITY"** *to the voice of the Holy Spirit.*

Firstly, I want you to understand the difference between *your permissive will and the perfect will of God for your life.*

The bible says in *1 Corinthians 3:11 For no other foundation can anyone lay than that which is [already] laid, which is Jesus Christ (the Messiah, the Anointed One).*

PERMISSIVE WILL IN CHOICE OF A SPOUSE: This arises when you make God to "understand/reason" your own choice based on your own criteria.

A typical example is a Brother 'A' mature and qualified enough to seek the face of God for a life partner; but in the course of his seeking, he felt delayed and decided to select Sister 'B' and thereafter presents her to the Pastor for prayers. Well the bible says if the foundation be destroyed, what can the righteous do? In this context, some Pastors obviously may tread with 'earthly wisdom' in order not to sound harsh if the Holy Spirit reveals negative or that they are not spiritually compatible, thereby ruining the future of these innocent singles. Anyway, let it be in your mind that if such brother/sister succeeds in such arrangement he has benefited from *the permissive will of God;*

- *I will bless whom I will bless.*
- *Your sins will be forgotten,*
- *Before they call, I will answer,*

He or the innocent lady might have pleased God at some point in life and that's the reward or might be the reward of either of their parents having pleased God (3rd or 4th generations away) and God decided to visit the blessing or compensation on Brother 'A' or sister 'B'.

THE PERFECT WILL OF GOD IN CHOOSING A PARTNER:

If Brother 'A' would consider the will of God in choosing his life partner; *(depending on his spiritual maturity and daily relationship with God)* he will either have received directly from the Holy Spirit *(with spiritual confirmation from his Pastor)* or would have referred his interest in Sister 'B' to his *Holy Spirit filled* Pastor for divine confirmation before personally approaching her.

Please note that your choice of a woman/man would either make or mare your future. So ensure you have the right man of God ministering into your life and future. If your spirit does not approve of his (pastor) personal life, do not involve him in your matrimony, even if he can preach or sing heaven down.

With this approach, the foundation of the relationship is already on the Rock of Ages. Remember, any home built on the Rock of Ages will always withstand all weather conditions without the world press/paparazzi coming to find out where, why and how have the failing couple arrived at a state of such embarrassing magnitude; should the accuser of brethren intrude into their home.

- **MY EXPERIENCE:** I have been in ungodly relationships *(even as an active Christian worker and a Minister)* until God showed me His mercy and such 'illicit affairs' came to a permanent end in my life.

Although, thereafter, the temptations were still pouring in, but my covenant as a prayer warrior and a servant in the Lord's vineyard tenaciously held me
- back, even at the height of satanic pressures and temptations. For these, I give God the glory, because *He said let he who thinks he stands take heed, lest he falls*. I can confidently say here that in those days of SSS - *(single and still searching)*, my song has

always been – ***'Do something new in my life oh Lord*................** as prophesied to me by one of my
• honoured fathers in the Lord – Late Prophet T.O. Obadare at CAC, Kings Cross, London in 2002.

On the day I noticed my wife, the Holy Spirit Ministered to me that I should request for a deliverance prayer from my colleagues in the Choir (Cliwom Sanctuary of Praise), they obliged and I knelt down while they prayed. Immediately after the Sunday morning choir prayer session and as I descended the stairs into the sanctuary for Sunday worship, the Holy Spirit ministered to me that He will open my eyes 'to behold something truly new'. ***Remember it is only in the presence of God that your godly aspirations can be fulfilled in absolute liberty.***

Reader, this real life story might sound funny to you, but our God performs His miracles through the Holy Spirit "suddenly". If it is not sudden, then, you already have a premonition and it is no longer a miracle, since you have planned for it.

As I entered the Sanctuary, I beheld the image of my "Jewel of an inestimable value" sitting next to one of the pillars in the church ***(a position which was almost considered her permanent sit then)*** and the Holy Spirit said, **"This is your wife"**. *It is worth mentioning here that many men and women of God have prophesied to me in Nigeria years back that my* *wife is abroad, but I reasoned they were all 'spiritually sick'. Even if I will relocate to anywhere in the world, would I have to go on air to announce my arrival or advertise for the position of "a God ordained wife"? I disapproved of such prophesies and went ahead with ungodly relationships occasioned by lust, flesh and environmental influences, even after arriving Europe.*

While I entered the Church auditorium, I couldn't belief myself as I was going to pick my usual seat at the Choristers' stand. Hey!! I reasoned again, I have never had anything to do with this lady, nor have I had cause to interact with her at any point. I have never had any reference point of her personality, her life aspirations and thoughts, believes!! What if she is engaged or married etc.? *I tried to pray this knowledge out of my mind, but the Holy Spirit still insisted - **that's her.*** As I got to my sit, I immediately alerted a friend in the church who rose up spontaneously on hearing my revelation and walked up to 'the lady' for a chat *(**ignoring my plea to keep his peace**).* Then I realised God's involvement. I began to imagine why this guy would want to bring such embarrassment unto me; as I have never had anything to do with this lady *(not even a chat)*; I was even wandering if she isn't someone else's wife, a mother, she looks too composed, well presented and matured for a typical single lady; anyway, lets see what happens if truly this is from the Holy spirit. In summary, subsequent events, involvement of a friend's wife and confirmations corroborated the involvement of God in my choice of life partner and I give Him the glory for ordering my steps. A wrong choice at that stage would have been nothing short of a proverbial disgrace; I would rather have preferred to remain unmarried for the rest of my life.

***Friend**!, you can also hear from God in your bid to choose a life partner, but you need strong self control and a discerning spirit to distinguish the voice of God from lust, infatuation, match-making, or otherwise. Temptations abound all over, especially with the advent of technology in costume designs, love of the flesh, feminist sexual schemes owing to the fulfilment of the scriptures concerning many ladies practically begging men to permit them to bear their names, evil and sinister desires, etc.*

Also, there are a number of 'sampling men' around town, who specialise in hopping from bed to bed and from sister to sister in the name of 'checking girls out' (even amongst the so called 'holy people' and children of God).

Now that you are born again, you *(as I have myself)* need to repent from all these, to hear from God as I have heard. It looks weird to some people but it is real and very possible.

I must say at this point that my waiting has given me the best lady any sane man could behold in his home. She is an embodiment of a 'real woman' and I give God all the glory. He said whoever finds a good wife finds favour in His sight. He said such a man will sit at the gate with elders and princes. She is extra priceless and a jewel of inestimable value.

Rev. Dr. Ebenezer Ajitena in one of his teachings on qualities of a real woman enunciated some of the foundational principles upon which an aspiring lady should build her personality and wrote that:

1. **A real woman is priceless -** *Prov. 31: 10-31*
2. **Trustworthy -** *Deborah*
3. **Is a gap-stander** *(A guide: I Tim. 5:14)*
4. **A hand-washer -** *Mary*
5. **A Home-maker –** *(Prov. 14:1)*
6. **A Home-keeper –** *(Titus 2: 4-5)*
7. **A Risk-taker -** *Esther*
8. **Highly submissive and faithful to God and her own husband –** *1ˢᵗ Pet. 3:1-2*

Finally, while he likened other women *(loose women on the streets)* to a motor car which can be driven by anyone *(even without a driver's licence)*, he said a real woman is *"a well"*.

The truth is, I eventually found mine after my over Twenty years (20years+) in the wilderness world of marital choice confusion, occasioned by external influences, lack of exposure and immaturity.

Proverbs 18:22 He who finds a [true] wife finds a good thing and obtains favour from the Lord. I give God the glory for granting me His divine favour in spite of my ugly marital antecedents.

BEWARE OF FRIENDS AND FAMILIES IN MAKING YOUR CHOICE

In making your choice *(after hearing from God)*, brother/sister, be convinced that you cannot explain any reason specifically why you have chosen 'this lady/brother' but the Holy Spirit has imposed him/her on you as the Lord's wish. Sit back, pray, find out who he/she is, alert your Pastor/Mentor *(who is not your friend, but cares for your well-being),* check out his/her *SWOT – strengths, weakness, opportunities in his/her life that can be tapped into, and the possible threats you have identified as anger, attitude, family pressures, self-centred visions, etc.,* build her up, *(while ladies encourage him to become),* design him/her to suit your life vision and aspirations; then take him/her for whatever he/she is – strong, weak, educated, uneducated, civilized, uncivilized, speaks queens English, speaks strong local African English, smart, dull, unlettered, lettered, healthy, frail, rich, poor, popular, unpopular, slim built, Fat, Tall, short, etc. As you carry the covenant of God (as Adam to Eve), you only need to identify a teachable spirit in her, (ladies be sure he has the fear of God, a life vision, loves God and available to serve Him, a reasonable and legitimate income and not necessarily a profession) and she/he will become whatever you want him/her to be in your life. We all cannot be professors, but you can be who God has designed you to be and still have professors on your payroll.

However, fiends in the image of friends would come up with their own perception of who your spouse should be, so that they can manipulate and have easy access into your home.

A fiend (*whom I have helped to build his own home*) even told me when I informed him of my choice and I quote, "Eh! You guy, how many years do you think you have to live that you have considered to be joined in marriage at this age *(mid forties)*? Are you sure you will live to eat the labour of your children?"

I immediately rejected this evil thought in the name of Jesus Christ; because I know God's plans for my life that I will not die but live to declare the goodness of the Lord in the land of the living where I have found myself, until I have fulfilled my divine purpose(s) on earth.

Some so called close pals also made futile efforts at dissuading my jewel of inestimable value from marrying me. She withstood them and they melted with their negative ideas. We jointly prayed on the destructive, debilitating and unfounded issues they have chosen to bring up at the eve of the 1st day my Pastor was to introduce us to our local church congregation.

Reader, <u>marriage is not for boys and girls but for matured and sound minded people who cannot be tossed around by opinions of so called 'well wishers'.</u>

Let it sink in your mind that your God given choice will always attract alternative ideas at the eve of your success, from 'well wishers'. ***Watch and pray.***

All you need in making your choice is God the Father, the Son and the Holy Spirit. Every other factor (including families) must be respected but come secondary *(if necessary at all)*.

If Prophet Hosea had listened to people's opinion, he would have missed God's purpose for his life; because *his wife was well known in the city for prostitution*. Even his parents (if they were both Popes) will object to his choice at that point.

No matter what he/she is, i.e. your spouse; if God has said it, accept it, move on and rely on Christ as your cornerstone. Worship God with all your heart and being.

Let others raise false evidences appearing real *(FEAR),* you just give out as much as God has given unto you, avoid friends of convenience, keep your home free of gossipers who are wolves in sheep skin and let the Holy spirit direct all your thoughts and actions, even when the one who wasn't part of your covenant with God has unsolicited alternatives.

YOUR CHOICE OF A LIFE PARTNER -
SHOULD BE PREMISED ON THE WORDS OF THE LORD; IN ORDER TO LIVE A LIFE THAT IS PLEASING TO GOD. (John 10:27)

The bible says in Isaiah 40:8 that grass withers, flowers fade, but the word of the Lord lives forever.

Bob Gordon *(in The Foundations of Christian Living)* posited that we can live a life that pleases God when we apply ourselves to the following:
a) Live a lifestyle that pleases God rather than ourselves or the people of the world *(1 John 2:15-17),*
b.) Make important for us what is important to Him (e.g. growing to be like Jesus, showing love to one

another and helping to fulfil the commission of Jesus Christ to make disciples for Him of all nations).

c.) Willingly take on God's burdens for the world, especially in prayer and evangelism, *(Matt. 6:9-10).*

d.) Willingly make sacrifices for God and even be willing to give up all if He asks us to, *(Mark 12:41-44).*

JESUS SAID *in– Mark 4:24*

"Be careful of what you are hearing. The measure [of thought and study] you give [to the truth you hear] will be the measure [of virtue and knowledge] that comes back to you – and more [besides] will be given to you who hear". (AMP)

WHO IS A LIFE PARTNER?

He or She is a person with whom you intend to spend whatever useful years God will permit you to live on earth; commencing from such a time, hour and date you commit yourself to having a God fearing and life-time loving/marital relationship with such a being, created in the image of God.

Nathan Olubiyi

PENGUIN DICTIONARY: An association involving close cooperation. A partner is also referred to as an associate in a joint venture.

AMPLIFIED BIBLE: *Amos 3:3 Can two walk together except they make appointment or be in agreement?*

NOTE: Coming together of two different persons involve concessions, loyalty, commitment, total decision to make things work amicably; and complete willingness to forget about self pride or individuality in decision making and principles.

Jesus taught us in *Matt. 20:26b-27 that "Whoever wants to be great among you must be a servant, 27. and whoever desires to be first among you must be your slave."*

The questions: Are you willing to be a worthy 'help-meet' to that man/woman you have chosen, so that you both can be 1st?

- **Do you belief with God all things are possible?** *(Matt. 19:26; Gen. 18:14; Job 42:2)*
- **Do you have faith and can endure?**
- **Are you timid? No, God has given you a sound mind.**

- Are you afraid? No, God has given you the spirit of boldness and courage.
- Would you close your ears to bystanders?
- Are you loaded with the fruits of the spirit? You are surely not perfect, but trust God for guidance,
- Have you considered your past before making your choice?
- Is he/she a person you can unconditionally forgive in the face of all odds? *(Matt 18:21-22)*
- Can you genuinely love him/her according to God's injunctions? *(Matt. 18:35)*
- Can you complement your partner?
- Are you a true salt of the earth?
- Are you spiritually prosperous? *(Matt. 5:9)*
- Can you pray yourself out of *(Matt. 10:36)* in your home?
- Can you share your very exclusive secrets with your proposed partner?
- What is your position on *Matt. 15:4* to your future in-laws?
- Will you be able and willing to abhor assumptions in your home?
- Can you both praise and worship God together in the beauty of His holiness,

even under the pressures of life? Then meditate on the lyrics of this song as written by *John Chandler –*

CHRIST IS OUR CORNERSTONE

1. *Christ is our corner-stone, on Him alone we build; with His true saints alone, the courts of heaven are filled; On His great love our hopes we place, of present grace and joy above.*

2. *O then with hymns of praise, these hallowed courts shall ring; our voices we will raise, the three in one to sing; and thus proclaim in joyful song, both loud and long, that glorious name.*

3. *Here, gracious God do thou, for evermore draw nigh; accept each faithful vow, and mark each suppliant sigh; In copious shower on all who pray; each holy day Thy blessings pour.*

4. *Here may we gain from heaven, the grace which we implore; and may that grace, once given, be with us evermore; until that day when all the blest, to endless rest are called away. Amen*

Chapter 5

WHAT IS MARRIAGE

ORIGIN OF MARRIAGE:

The Author – God
The factors involved in Godly marriage – Male and Female
Fruits of marriage – Children
Influences on marriage - include family, friends, children, Associates, Governments, Religious Institutions and Associations, self-belief and various schools of thoughts. All these could either have positive or negative influences on individual homes.

Many confuse Marriage with Wedding or they use these distinct words interchangeably. However, I will try to give a clearer picture to the potential single who I belief needs to know more about these words and their significance in the life of every human being.

In context, **the Author of marriage after creation** "saw that all He created was good" from *Genesis 1-2:verse 17* but realised a need as in *Gen. 2:18 And the Lord God said, It is not good that the man should be alone; I will make him an help meet for him.* Some versions of the Holy Scripture said "helper". Though realising Adam was not lonely in the Garden of Eden, His intention was to make or create Adam "a companion" with whom he could easily relate as opposed to relating to beasts and fowls as "friends" to avert being "alone" in thoughts and actions; implying or meaning "animals were not designed by their maker to be friends to humans"; reason why zoo beasts and domesticated beasts could still harm their keepers at a point in their lives, even after feeding them with all supposed "usual meals".

The Author of marriage formed Adam to till the ground and name all He had created. He later created Eve to make him a reliable and worthy "support" not necessarily a "housemaid or equal" after He gave instruction not to meddle with some fruits from certain trees in the Garden of Eden. See *Gen. 2:16-17 before He thought of making Eve in verse 18.*

Note: God's intention for marriage was primarily for companionship and later "multiplication, replenishment of the Earth and dominion over everything He had created" (*See **Gen. 1:28***) not child bearing through labour, which He had to command and permit through copulation after "the great fall" to satisfy our flesh and to fulfil His curse on Eve in *Gen. 3:16.*

He also intended man to be the head of marriage while the woman is required to submit to the will of her own man (not Pastor's or other people's wills). *See I Pet. 3:1-6.*

In verse 7 of the same book – I Pet. 3, He permitted and instructed man through His Apostle to relate with our "divine companions" with Godly love, wisdom and knowledge; not academic or worldly knowledge as it obtains today in many homes. These were followed with further instructions on how best to build Godly homes.

MARRIAGE AUTHOR'S INTENTION IN SUMMARY: was for Adam to have a "helper". See *Gen. 2:17-21* "AND NOT AN EQUAL MATE" as the world of civilization has made us to believe today.

Wedding defined – It is a ceremony scheduled for a day to celebrate the coming together of two distinct personalities for companionship and co-habitation – *Nathan Olubiyi*.

Marriage starts on the next day after wedding; when every well –wishers would have begun their home journeys, merriments and dancing ended, you will now begin to see the real person in your spouse who poses, changes steps, paints face with all sorts of colourings, speaks like he has never been to the toilet nor snores.

Marriage is an opportunity for you to be lifted **up** by a (supposed) trusted partner (until he/she proves otherwise) in your quest to fulfil your divine purpose on earth with whom you can one day say- God we thank you for your mercies and faithfulness.

__Marriage is a God ordained companionship__ and co-habitation premised on the fulfilment of divine order on helping one another, in fruitfulness and multiplication.

__Marriage is a companionship built on the everlasting Rock of Ages and mutual trust.__ The contractual element *(wedding ceremony)* which the people of the world now consider to be a sine-qua-non is only a physical confirmation to those who will say hosanna today or crucify him tomorrow. This is necessary in order to acquaint them with the fact that you are neither available to their pranks nor their user scheming.

__It is an institution where you cling to your partner in all intents and purposes for the fulfilment of God's purposes for your home/family;__ while every other being must come in or be involved only when invited to do so.

__Marriage is synonymous to food and water__ – this is because we can hardly separate ourselves from this institution, either as a father, a mother, a son, or a daughter. No one has ever dropped from the sky (even our Lord Jesus Christ came by the unction and descent of the Holy Spirit upon mother Mary who was then already considering marriage with Joseph). 'Water and food makes up the human being after divine creation from dust' and they are a direct reflection of who we are, just as marriage to our home.

It is the only Divine institution on earth that can never be obliterated: *S*o long as there will be man in existence, even animals mate to reproduce (though we may say as per the limit of our knowledge of creation, maybe not in marriage anyway). Be prepared for regular mutually enjoyable sexual activities *(premised on the knowledge of the word of God)* in order not to subject your spouse to unnecessary temptations.

In Marriage, the scripture says the man is the head of the house as Christ is the head of the church, while the woman is a worthy helpmate and not a slave or an inferior personality. *Please read my spiritual grand father's book on Understanding the power of Women by Dr. Myles Munroe for better analysis of the personality of women.*

Marriage is an institution where every stakeholder train and develop with time. There is no best marriage anywhere. It only takes the grace of God, tolerance, regular M.O.T. as re-assurance check, no individuality, mutual respect and will power for the home to succeed.

Marriage is a companionship premised on Christ, trust and the will power to make a companionship last' till death do us part' and not for the sake of earthly wealth as money, fame, achievements, etc.

The contractual element (wedding ceremony) which the people of the world now consider to be a sine-qua-non is only a physical confirmation to those who will say hosanna today or crucify him tomorrow. This is necessary in order to acquaint them with the fact that you are neither available to their pranks nor their user scheming.

In understanding the divine purpose of Marriage, partners (to be) should appreciate the fact that the corporate success of any society would only depend on how successful our matrimonies are, and how well we apply ourselves to the divine foundational principles of *Male – Female companionship and co-habitation* as detailed in the bible, not academic postulations of what marriage is to the unbeliever - ***Nathan. Olubiyi***

FAMILY CREED

Ephe 3:16-19 May He grant you out of the rich treasury of His glory to be strengthened and reinforced with mighty power in the inner man by the [Holy] Spirit [Himself indwelling your innermost being and personality]. 17. May Christ through your faith [actually] dwell (settle down, abide, make His permanent home) in your hearts! May you be rooted in deep love and founded securely on love.
18. That you may have the power and be strong to apprehend and grasp with all saints [God's devoted people, the experience of that love] what is the breadth and length and height and depth [of it]. 19. [That you may really come] to know [practically, through

experience for yourselves] the love of Christ, which far surpasses mere knowledge [without experience]; that you may be filled [through all your being] unto all the fullness of God [may have the richest measure of the divine presence, and become a body wholly filled and flooded with God Himself. (AMP)

God's mind about "Humility in Marriage"

The only person God hates is the proud man or woman. He loves every sinner, He cares for them, He gives them opportunities of 'another chance'; He does not want them dead but for them to repent of their sins and become Holy as He is Holy, as much as they humanly can.

Matt. 18:4 *Therefore, whoever humbles himself like this child is the greatest in the kingdom of heaven. (NIV)*
Rom. 12:3 *for by the grace given Me I say to every one of you: Do not think of yourself more highly than you ought, but rather think of yourself with sober judgement, in accordance with the measure of faith God has given you. (NIV)*

Experience: A vivid study on my mentors' lives, books and ministrations have taught me a lot of benefits derivable from being humble.

A lot of men and women divinely designed for greatness have missed it and lost their chances to pride. If I had presented myself as a former worker and Minister in the Redeemed Christian Church of God (Gloryland Assembly, London) in my new church; probably, I would have been unable to learn all I have learnt in those years that I have been in the Ministry. I had to abase myself, open my heart up to learning more, serve and worship God in truth and in spirit. All these endeared me to the heart of the set man of God in the house and he's been a great blessing to my life.

I am sure, God also considered my obedience and service before giving me my choice of a woman, all to His glory alone.

The Personality of our Lord Jesus Christ in Humility: He chose to live a sinless life in honour of others as you and I. *Matt. 16:21-25*

Chapter 6

"CHOICE" DEFINED

The Penguin English Dictionary defines **"CHOICE"** as the act of choosing, of high quality, selected with care and well chosen.

The Oxford Advanced Learner's Dictionary defines **"CHOICE"** as an act of choosing between two or more possibilities – *of very good quality but not the highest quality.*

SCRIPTURAL POSITION ON "CHOICE"

The Lord – *"From all the fruit in this garden you may freely eat; but the fruit of life and death, thou shall not eat. For if you do, you shall surely die".* (Gen. 2:16-17)

Jesus Christ – *said, "I have lain before you life and death; but I encourage you to take life."*

Matt. 18:19 Again I tell you, if two of you on earth agree (harmonize together, make a symphony together) about whatever [anything and everything] they may ask, it will come to pass and be done for them by My Father in heaven. (AMP)

So we are all given the express grace of making choice on daily basis and in all we do; but note the 'great power in agreement'. It is so powerful that God had to call on the Hosts of heaven to join Him in going down to the world to confuse the language of those who decided to build the Tower of Babel to reach the heavens, before their dreams were truncated; else it would have been achieved. For further studies, digest: ***Gen. 11:1-9, Amos 3:3***

Reader, if your choice of man or woman is of God, he/she will be obedient to Godly principles, he/she will be loyal to you in love, Christ will be the cornerstone of your relationship- not sex, money, children, fame or family ties.

He/she will only be for God and you, while every other person(s) remain on the sideline as spectators/well-wishers at all times. Then whatever you both shall agree upon shall become manifest and before you call, the Lord Almighty will answer. ***See 1 Pet. 3:7.***

Spouses who base their relationship on Money, Sex, fruit of the womb and fame, family ties *(as what is your father's position in the society or church)* have missed it and it will be extremely difficult for them to flow in the spirit while all these conditions fail.

If you come across any single (male/female) whose emphasis is on any of these fleshy considerations; flee as he/she is an appearance of evil. I have written this because I was once at cross-roads like you *(may be)*, thinking whatever I have done is the best and my fleshy wish was the determinant of my choice of relationships. Now I am of age and I have dropped such schools of thought for Godly living.

WHAT IS DIVINE CHOICE OF LOVE?

I Corr. 13:4-8 "Love is patient, kind, does not boast, not proud, does not envy, not rude, not self-seeking and not easily angered. It keeps no record of wrongs. Love does not delight in evil but rejoices with the truth. It always protects trusts, always hopes, and always perseveres. Love never fails".

SENSITIVITY AND INSENSITIVITY
(Understanding the voice of God and His will for our lives).

-His voice could come to us in our dreams *(Matt. 1:20-21),*
-He could speak to us through the advices and counsel of His anointed men and women *(Prov. 12:15)* even through 'donkeys'

-Through visions *(Acts. 10:9-18),*

-By gifts of the spirit, e.g. words of wisdom, prophecy, tongues, words of knowledge, *(1 Cor.12:4-11)*

Devise divine ways of testing spirits

Ref. Verses: 1 Cor. 14:29; 1 John 4:1 - Test all spirits to discern who is actually speaking to you; before you take any life committing decision. If any prophesy does not come as a confirmation of what God has already placed on your heart and it comes as a surprise, be very careful. Do not let mere circumstance or sweet talk run your lives; as this could permit Satan into your lives with ease.

Characteristics of divinely Chosen words

➢ **They are immediate – very powerful and arresting. The have 'live current' in them.**
➢ **They are very relevant – applies to our situation in application and timeliness,**
➢ **They are effective – Fruitful,**
➢ **They are fitting – Consistent with other witnesses around our lives and circumstances.**

SENSITIVITY:

The **Penguin English Dictionary** says - capable of being stimulated or excited by external agents such as light, gravity or contact. It went further to assert sensitivity as being finely aware of the attitudes and feelings of others or of subtleties of a work of art.

Oxford Dictionary – Aware of and being able to understand other people and their feelings.

SCRIPTURAL SENSITIVITY

In furtherance to our discussion on discernment and testing of spirits, the bible encourages us to be very sensitive to things of the spirit in build-up to our faith. We are enjoined to be sensitive to signs of time and spiritual indicators as revealed in the bible, in the management of our life endeavours on daily basis.
Ref. verse: Heb. 11:6, James 1:5 our God is always willing to reveal Himself to us: but the level of faith we have in Him and sinful nature determines our sensitivity and reaction to His promptings.

Chapter 7

Trials and Temptation

One of my spiritual mentors ***Rev. (Dr.) E.O. Ajitena*** in his book ***[Secrets of the tempter]*** wrote that ***"the tempter is one who tempts to reveal weaknesses."*** Obviously the devil will never attack you by your strength but by those areas of your life that you are always struggling with.

However, you must appreciate the fact that, not all temptations originate from the devil's camp. Some are deliberately designed by God to affirm your stand or to establish if you truly love, trust or place your hope in Him as the everlasting Rock of Ages.

Dr. Valerie Willman, a licensed clinical psychologist, board certified in Christian Counselling and residing on the beautiful island of Kauai, Hawaii. Dr. Willman's book, **Victory over Cancer: Live as Though It Were True... Because It Is!** When asked what inspires her, she answered that 'it is people who decide to "live their life as though God's Word were true" —those who don't accept the doctor's report, but instead rely on the scripture ***Isaiah 54:17*** that promises "no weapon formed against you will prosper". She told the story of how her husband Mark came to Christ, during a time of marital separation.

He inspired her because he believed against all hope that their marriage would be restored-- and it was!'

What sort inspiration comes from you in your own personal days of Temptation in your marriage, within your family, friends and colleagues?

Asking her why she wrote this book; Dr. Willman said "I didn't write it—God did! You can read my college dissertation to know—I can't write! But God laid it on my heart, and it was confirmed by so many that I had to share my story. Not to make money, but to touch lives. If just one person is encouraged and inspired to trust God and put Him to the test by living as though it were true, then I have fulfilled God's purpose in writing this book. It's all about encouragement and being an instrument used by the Lord!"

Read the book of Job for a proper understanding of God's temptation. He (God) said He will never tempt us beyond what we can contain and He will even make ways of escape for us in such situations.

So, when you seem to be tempted or in your wilderness situations, know that the Lord is with you. He will neither leave nor forsake you. Job said, 'even though He slays me yet will I trust in Him'.

Arthur Wallis: *(Living God's way) says "Over the past 2000 years the word 'temptation' has undergone a change in meaning. It once meant both 'testing' and 'seducing to evil'; thus has a positive and negative significance. The positive side is that temptation is a testing of our lives as permitted by God, with the intent of producing spiritual growth. The negative side is that temptation is Satan's seductive enticing of the believer to live contrary to God's plan for his life".*

INSENSISTIVITY- *Origins of Temptation by: Bob Gordon*

Satan tempts us in many ways including:
- Encouraging love of money *(John 12:6)*
- Encouraging sexual immorality *(Gen. 39:7-10)*
- Encouraging disobedience *(Gen. 31:1-7)*
- Boasting/pride in our earthly achievements *(Acts. 12:21-23)*
- Encouraging grumbling, murmuring and gossiping *(1 Cor. 10:10; Col. 3:8-9).*
- Encouraging us to love things or people rather than God first *(Malch.4:9)*

PURPOSE OF TRIALS AND TEMPTATIONS - *James 1:2-3, Job 1:12, Job 2:6, Job 42:1-17*

1. They show us what we truly are if we have the opportunity.

2. They are designed to assist in the preparation of our lives to receive the good things God desires to give us.

3. They expose our weaknesses so that we can discover where we need God's strength and grace.

4   They are allowed by God to come upon us in order to:
    - Refine us *(Psalm 66:10)*
    - Check our foundations *(1 Cor. 3:10-15)*
    - Humble, discipline and teach us *(Deut. 8:2-5)*
    - Remove what can be shaken off from us *(Heb. 12:25-29)*
    - Strengthen our little faith *(1 Pet. 1:6-7)*
    - Enable us to be an over-comer *(Rev. 2&3)*
    - Develop perseverance which, when it finishes its work, yields us maturity, completeness and no lack of anything *(James 1:2-4), (Book of Job)*

HOW TO DEAL WITH TEMPTATION

1. By using the word of God as Jesus did *(Matt. 4:1-11) – The power of "it is written"*.
2. By a deliberate decision and act of will *(1 Pet. 2:11; Prov.4:14-15)*
3. By being watchful *(Matt. 6:41; Mark 14:38) Keep your spiritual eyes open.*
4. By submitting to God and resisting the devil *(James 4:7)*
5. Not giving Satan any opportunity or opening in your life and home *(Ephe.4:27)*
6. By cultivating in increasing measure - faith, goodness, knowledge of God's word, self-control, perseverance, godliness, brotherly kindness and agape love *(2 Pet. 1:5-9)*
7. By putting on your spiritual armour to enable you stand against the devil's schemes *(Ephe. 6:10-18)*
8. By looking on to Jesus who was once tempted in all respects as we are *(Heb. 4:15).* He is therefore well positioned to help us to overcome temptation as He did *(Heb. 2:18).*

He is therefore well positioned to help us to overcome temptation as He did Heb. 2:18 For because He Himself [in His humanity] has suffered in being tempted (tested and tried), He is able [immediately] to run to the cry of (assist, relieve) those who are being tempted and tested and tried [and who therefore are being exposed to suffering].

SATAN'S POSITION ON PRAYER

Satan and his demons are not creative; but can cremate creativity through weariness, tiredness, discouragement, back-biting others, pride, love of money and position, self-aggrandisement, unconfessed sins, fornication, adultery, false prophets, lying, murderous acts, etc. *He (the devil) knows:*

- **Prayer works and it brings the power of God into believers' lives as disciples of Jesus Christ.**
- **Praying people can resist the devil and defeat his purposes when they understand the authority they have in Christ.** *(James 4:7; 1 Pet. 5:8-9)*
- **Satan will not catch those who watch and pray off guard** *(Matt. 26:41)*
- **Prayer brings about God's will and thwarts Satan's will.**

Satan's Tools on children of God -

- **Distractions,**
- **Temptations – covetousness, illicit sex, greed,**
- **Ungodly thoughts,**
- **Condemnation,**
- **Encouragement of doubt,**

- Fear and despair,
- Unforgiveness, – *Mark 11:25*
- Laziness, – *James 4:2*
- Wrong motives, – *James 4:3*
- Unconfessed sin, *(1 John 1:7-9; Isa. 59:1,2)*

WHY PRAYERS ARE NOT ANSWERED

Our Jehovah Jireh loves us so much that He is always present and willing to meet all our needs. This was established in the book of *Dan. 10:12-14* --- Fear not...... Your prayers have been answered the first time.

All He (God) wants from us is to have faith in Him and pray - *Mark 10:12-14*

Hindrances to answered prayers: Things God hates – *Prov. 6:16, 17-19, 25, 32, 34*

1. *Unconfessed sin – 1ˢᵗ John 1:9* …If we confess our sins, He is faithful and just enough to forgive us of our sins

2. *Hatred – 1ˢᵗ John 2:9-11* – vengeance and retaliation (Naboth and his vineyard- *1ˢᵗ Kings 21)*

3. *Love of the world – 1st John 2:15-17* – deceit and lying

4. *Dislike for the knowledge of God's word – 1st John 2:5*

5. *Unforgiveness - Mark 10:25*

6. *Carnal Mindedness – Rom. 8:6*, The bible says the things of God are foolishness to the carnal minded. *Proverbs 13* also emphasized on the need for us to nurture our children early enough (V.24) for us to have peace when we become old.

7. *Haters of knowledge and greatness – Prov. 21:6* – Unrepentant spirit

8. *Fear* – The Lord empowered Elijah but he ran away for Jezebel – *1st Kings 19*. Fear God but respect your fellow man/woman old or young.

9. *Jealousy and Negative anointing* – Cain and Abel

10. *Pride* – Satan and the fallen Angels.

11. *Poor time Management* – Ecclesiastes says there the time for everything on earth. Even God was sensitive to time in creation and in all He does, because He is not a God of confusion.

12.   *Spiritual depression and Unbelief* – Spirit of religion and false religion.

13.   *Impatience and the spirit of Anti-Christ* – lawlessness and disobedience.

14.   *Adultery and Fornication* - Spirit of Seduction

15.   *Discouragement and compromise* – Long time waiting without results

SPIRITS THAT HINDER PRAYERS IN THE CHURCH: Re: Joshua the high priest was followed into the Lord's presence by the accuser – Satan. *Zechariah 3:1 Then [the guiding angel] showed me Joshua the high priest standing before the Angel of the Lord, and Satan standing at Joshua's right hand to be his adversary and to accuse him.*

a.   **Spirit of Jezebel** – Killer of prophetic ministries. Prosperity of the wicked is for a while – *1st Kings 21*

b.   **Spirit of Esau** – Sellers of birth-right for food and money

c.   **Spirit of Manasseh** – Transferred blessings

d.   **Spirit of Pisgah** – Almost there but never there

e.   **Spirit of Saul** – From Prophet to dinning with witch of Endor

f.   **Spirit of Pharaoh** – Stubborn pursuer

g. **Spirit of Herod** – Spirit that kills blessing at infancy

h. **Pharisee Spirit** – Mr. Know-all – holier than thou

MANAGEMENT OF DIFFERENCES IN HOMES.

Possible causes of domestic violence:

1. Immaturity and lack of exposure to the understanding of gender value systems –
Amos 3:3,

2. Permitting undue/unsolicited intervention of third parties in your family issues,

3. Backgrounds, associated assumptions and religious believes,

4. Lack of Trust and attitudes which may encourage suspicion,

5. Inadequate fun and sexual activities –
1 Cor. 7:1-5,

6. Communication failure – *Prov.18:13,*

7. Unrealised dreams and assumptions –
   Prov. 23:18,

8. Bad Temperaments and unsettled arguments –
   Col. 3:18-19,

9. Inconsiderate work/business schedules,

10. Secret extra marital activities and undue separation,

11. Inadequate prayer life,

12. Lacking knowledge of the word of life,

13. Societal norms and Regulations,

14. Money and material things,

15. Different life aspirations, vision or goals.

Rev. Solomon Adebara *(Nigerian)* introducing his book ***Conflicts and Resolutions in Marriage*** posited that "no couple ever goes to the altar to solemnize their marriage contract with the mind of failing".

I would rather say, no genuine child of God will ever go into marriage with the mind of failing. At least we have witnessed instances *(especially in the so called civilized world or 'nations where Satan lives')* where marriages are premised on earthly family contract laws, status and subject to flow of regular funds, etc.

Before you go into a Holy marriage, be prepared and be willing to drop who you used to be; may be, a non-conformist, a night crawler, an extrovert or an introvert, smooth/erudite talker or speaker, reservist or a shy personality. You may even be a Pastor or Bishop, your home is surely different from your congregation.

You must find a way of developing your own ***Home norms*** to suit your home visions in line with God's plan and not what obtains in your parent's settings, your church or the societal dictates, no matter how affluent or 'supposedly civilised' your background may be. Neither should it be what obtains in your friend's home; *who may be a drug dealer, a fraudulent manipulator or an armed robber.*

You have to be a new person entirely – Col 3: 9-17 *lie not one to another, seeing that ye have put off the old man with his deeds; and have put on the new man, which is renewed in knowledge after the image of Him that created him.*

I implore you to make up your mind considering all the afore-mentioned possible causes of differences in homes. Open up your mind and be willing to allow things work with a renewal of your mind, not minding your father's wealth as compared with what your spouse has to offer; your status in the secular world which may confine you to certain highly professional conversations completely alien to your spouse.

What obtains in your parents' home, if unscriptural must be dropped immediately you make up your mind on walking the aisle with your life partner?

Christian ladies, be prepared to give the exact honours you will give your church Pastor or Bishop to your husband in greater love.

Christian bachelors, be prepared to love your spouse with the sound understanding that they are of a weaker sex, regular receivers who may sometimes over–stretch issues, mostly flexible, have eyes for details where you over-look things and they want to have your attention at all times.

Apparently, regular *(though seemingly uncomfortable)* adjustments have to be made in order to save your home. This price if unpaid could make room for loose girls or loose men taking over the reigns of your home.

Chapter 8

CONCLUSION

Marriage institution was established by God and not man nor technology.

For anyone to be successful in marriage, you have to apply yourselves to the sections relevant to Marriage in our spiritual manual – *The bible.*

Put on the image and armour of God in all you intend to achieve in your marriage. Be prepared for the devil any day.

Do not be unequally yoked with an unbeliever in marriage. He/she will hurt your soul all through your life, if not ordained by God to either train you or draw your spouse to the Kingdom. *Seek God's approval first.*

Avoid individualism in your daily relationship with your spouse. This will breed a time bomb which leads to divorce.

Share *(reasonably)* those issues that may benefit and concern your spouse.

Avoid excluding your spouse from plans which may affect you both.

Plan to open up your financial and moral situations.

- ***Heb. 4:15** The bible says " for we do not have a high priest (Jesus) who is unable to sympathise with our weaknesses, but we have one who has been tempted in every way, yet without sin.*
- **Flee from all appearances of Evil,**
- **Resist the devil and he shall flee,**
- ***1 Cor. 10:13** "No temptation has seized you except what is common to man. And God is faithful; He will not let you be tempted beyond that which you can bear. But when you are tempted, He will also provide a way out so that you can stand up under it.*

Friend! Be sensitive in and out of season, the enemy lurks around looking for whom he may devour. Make sure you are daily loaded with the fruits of the spirit of God and it shall be well with you. Amen.

For over 20 years, I have made costly marital mistakes; I have since learnt to stop trusting in man, no matter how close he/she may be. ***They will make you fail and turn around to blame you for your foolishness.*** Even those who should listen and learn while you talk, will come as 'angel of light' ***(in*** *despise and concealed hatred)* to advise you on how you can keep your home in marriage.

Be sensitive, plan to build a good wall of privacy in your marriage and pray very well for God's direction before you choose your life partner.

Kindly bear in mind that mine is a restored mind better positioned to write about Christian choices in preparation for marriage because I have failed more than twice.

A man/woman who made his/her choice and have lived under the same roof *(even for 80 years in peace);* most often, may not appreciate the spiritual, emotional and physical implications of making wrong choices in marriage. Some will even believe in themselves to be excellent husbands or wives 'who knows and better understands how to relate with the opposite sex'. They are only experienced in harmonious living and not the understanding of God's will in opposite sex choice making for a Kingdom Home on earth.

Marital choice costly mistakes *(when made)* could amount to a source of significant life set-back in all ramifications. It has taken me 20years+ to find my marital bearing.

Chapter 9

FOOD FOR THOUGHT – LIVE SEEMS TO ME 'A GAME OF CHOICE' WHERE YOU SUCCEED ONLY BY GOD'S GRACE AND ACCEPTANCE OF YOUR GOD GIVEN WILL-POWER.

1. **A CHOICE ENCOUNTER**: the only way things are going to change for you is when you change within the unknown but specified time allotted to you to be alive. Can you explain how you fought the battle in your mother's womb to overcome other over 2 million contenders to be fertilised?

2. **LIVE A LIFE OF GOOD HEALTH:** You should make sure that the outside of you is a good reflection of the inside of you; *Be in good health as your soul prospereth,*

3. **THE GIFT OF RELATIONSHIPS:** Time, effort and imagination must be summoned constantly to keep any relationship flourishing and growing – Does your association with a person or

class of persons challenge you to become great or are they friends of convenience? If you perceive emotional bareness and self-centeredness, disassociate yourself amicably. Love the Lord in truth and in spirit and let this transcend to your earthly God glorifying relationships,

4. **ACHIEVE YOUR GOALS:** The major reason for setting a goal is for what it makes of you to accomplish it; you cannot change your destination overnight, but you can change your direction overnight; Choose where you want to go and then build out your plan towards getting there. Never run on anybody's track, so that you will not die another man's death. Think deep, conceive your own vision and implement it with a divine blue-print from God. Be unique and not one who wait for others to be copied, before reasoning.

5. **MAKE PROPER USE OF YOUR TIME:** Everyday has many opportunities, but only one best opportunity – Discipline weighs ounces while regret weighs tons. If you do not design your own life plan, chances are you will fall into someone else's plan and they will plan for you to be reliant on them for your life survival. The

book of Ecclesiastes says there is time of everything on earth, check out for time wasting friends or associates, drop them amicably and move on with your life.

6. **IDENTIFY AND SURROUND YOURSELF WITH THE BEST PEOPLE:** Do not join any easy crowd; you won't grow. Go where the expectations and the demands to perform are higher. Surround yourself with divine winners, successful people who exhibit and live consistent to values and skills you want to acquire,

7. **MAKE A HONEST ASSESSMENT OF THOSE AROUND YOU:** Who are you around? What effect are they having on you? What have they got you doing or reading? What have they got you saying? Where do they have you going? What do they have you thinking? What do they have you becoming? **Place every individual into one of these 3 categories: Disassociation, limited association and expanded association, Ask yourself what amount of time with each person will challenge you to become the kind of person you want?**

8.   **CHALLENGE YOURSELF TO BECOME:** To attract attractive people you must be attractive. To attract powerful people you must be powerful, to attract committed people you must be committed. 'If you become, you can attract',

9.   **OPEN YOURSELF UP TO NEW KNOWLEDGE:** Desire knowledge about the word of God, how the world works, how your business/profession works, how to better your relationships. When you open yourself to vast new reasonable networks, their friends become your friends; soon your whole business and sphere of influence will change for the better,

10.   **CHECK YOUR ATTITUDE AND EMOTIONS ALWAYS:** Your attitude determines your altitude *(E.O. Ajitena).* Attitude is greatly shaped by influence and association. Who you hang around with will be a major determining factor in what your attitude becomes. 99% of your life success depends on your attitude and reactions to environmental influences. They will surely come from all directions.

11.	**BE A LIFE-LONG LEARNER:** *Formal education will make you a living while self education will make you a fortune.* Learning is the beginning of wealth, it is the beginning of health, and it is the beginning of spirituality. Searching learning is where the life success miracle process all begins,

12.	**ALL ABOUT LIFE IS SALES:** One key to having influence with others is to have others perceive you as a person of talent and virtue. Be a person of strong character and increasing skill and you will always be growing your influence.

Thomas Jefferson says, 'There is a natural aristocracy among men, the grounds of which is talent and virtue'.

Rev. (Dr.) Ebenezer Ajitena says, *(as broken down in my own words)* your skills and talents will make ways for you so much that those who have deliberately chosen to hate you will be compelled by the authority of natural aristocracy to admire and unconsciously favour you. Identify yours and display it to glorify God and for the benefit of the world you find yourself.

13. **INCOME SELDOM EXCEEDS PERSONAL DEVELOPMENT:** Whatever you desire to become directly influences what you get. You need to love what you will become, not money. *Whoever loves money never has money enough. Strive to work for yourself as profits are better than wages.* Ninety-nine percent of the wealthy became wealthy by serving themselves, investing wisely and capturing profits. Choose between the pain of discipline and the pain of regrets. *Your so called city employment income today is only 'an exploiter's assessment of your worth'.* They will only pay you a fraction of what you have made for them; but if the business is yours, you will determine what is due to you and your household.

14. **COMMUNICATION:** It brings the common ground for mutual understanding. It connotes 2 or more people working together to find common grounds of understanding. And whenever they find that common ground, they are positioned to have tremendous power and greater achievements together. Learn to

communicate clearly, interpret your proverbs, ask to clarify your assumptions.

15. **THE WORLD NEEDS ONE MORE LEADER:** The world is waiting for you and can always use more than one leader anyway. To lead others rightly, help them to change their thoughts, beliefs and actions for the better. Show them what you possess that should compel them to believe you are better and can be considered unique.

Jim Rohn says, '***The challenge of leadership** is to be strong, but not rude; be kind but not weak; be bold but not a bully; be thoughtful but not lazy, be humble but not timid; be proud but not arrogant, have humour but without folly'*.

VISION: As a good leader, you need to *develop an optimistic vision* – Know where you are and design a better destination for yourself.

- Create a positive vision of your future, consult with God only, and develop your plan to get there, communicate the already baked version to your Elizabeth, take advice and then execute the plan. *Mary was already pregnant of our Messiah before visiting Elizabeth. Do not visit your*

16. **LEAVE A POSITIVE LEGACY WHENEVER YOU CHOOSE TO MOVE ON:** Live a life that will help others spiritually, intellectually, physically, financially and relationally. Live a life that serves as an example of what an exceptional life can look like.

- We are but breezes of wind that blows through this World. Here one day, gone the next. No one knows how long he/she will live.
- You cannot choose how long you will live, but you can choose how well you will live,
- We can make a living or we can design a life no matter the level of afflictions – Emotional, spiritual, financial or otherwise,
- We must live out the philosophies we passionately believe in and have been sharing with others,
- Take time to help others and to teach them if they are teachable and willing to learn. Be patient, loving and loyal,

- Let others lead small lives, but not you. Let others argue over small things, but not you. Let others cry over small hurts, but not you. Let others leave their future in someone else's hands, but not you.

- *YOU HAVE YOUR WHOLE LIFE AHEAD OF YOU, LIVE IT TO THE FULLEST OF YOUR POTENTIALS. CHALLENGE YOUR INNATE PROPENSITY TO SUCCEED.*

Compiled in Dec.2005 with Inspiration from Jim Ron

Chapter 10

INSPIRATIONAL THOUGHTS

> **Search for the Hero inside you; let no man eulogise you.** Their principles are premised on hosanna today; crucify him tomorrow. When they can use you they sing your praises; else they search for your historical faults to nail you. Your good deeds are written on water while your mistakes are written on brass.

> **Be yourself and fulfil only God's plan for your life** while you are capable of doing so. Remember your God while you are young, before the evil days roll inn.

> **Never expect anyone** *(except appointed by God)* **to share your vision; always expect them to discourage you,** contemplate your failure or steal your ideas. Their cunning smiles are never the true intents of their minds.

> **Flee from every self centred friend,** relation (blood or otherwise) or acquaintances; because the manifestation of your glory, and breakthrough will make them hate you the

more. Cling to those who share and sincerely encourage your vision only.

➢ **Trust, rely on, have confidence in and reverence God only,** because He is the only one in possession of your manufacturer's manual. Every other creature will only relate to you on personal perceptions; which have nothing to do with God's plans for you. Respect everyone *(including the younger ones)*.

➢ In all, **seek ye first the Kingdom of God and His righteousness;** thereafter every other thing as life pleasures, money, wealth, fame, propensity to acquire everything to yourself and family alone will come from the promises of God that you should try Him with your substance and you will see Him opening His heavenly windows to pour you *a blessing* that you will not have enough room to contain.

➢ Soak yourself and your household always in the blood of Jesus Christ. *The enemy you think is far away is just within your family.* No distant enemy can succeed or prevail over your life without an accomplice enemy within.

The bible says the Lord has exalted Him *(Jesus Christ)* so much that He has given Him a name that is above every other name, that at the mention of His name, every knee must bow and every tongue confess that Jesus is Lord. Even of the creatures in the air, on land and in the sea. So, all He requires of you is a daily confession of His Lordship.

➢ Always decree with the power of the Almighty God against every enchantment, plans, strategies, incursions, judgements and divination of your spiritual enemies *(whether you belief or not; I know they are real)* who if permitted, will becloud your reasoning and may want you to make mistake in your choice of a life partner; just because they have seen your God ordained future glory.

As I belief you have read this book with divine understanding, please pray to the LORD (your Owner) to give you the exact desire of your heart in Marriage and so shall it be in Jesus name, Amen.

Prayer Points:

1. Oh Lord! Open my spiritual eye and give me a receptive heart to appreciate that person whom you have destined for me in Jesus name.

2. Father, touch my spirit to discern the right personality of my bone of bone and flesh of flesh in Jesus name.

3. I will not be joined in marriage with a strange man (woman) who will deny me the Kingdom of God in Jesus mighty name.

RESOURCES

- *The Amplified Bible*
- *The Holy Bible (KJV)*
- *The Message Bible*
- **Secrets of the Tempter** *by Rev. E.O. Ajitena*
- **The Foundations of Christian Living** *by Bob Gordon with David Fardouly*
- **What Men Really Want and Desires In a Woman-** *Dr. Myles Munroe*
- **Walking in Divine Favour** *by Jerry Savelle*
- **The Penguin English Dictionary.**
- **The Oxford Advanced Learners Dictionary.**
- **Conflict Resolution in Marriages** *– Rev. Solomon Adebara.*
- **Abraham Maslow's Hierarchy of Needs (1954***)** *- www.simplypsychology.org*

"Blessed be God, even the Father of our Lord Jesus Christ, the Father of mercies, and the God of all comfort; Who comforteth us in all our tribulation, that we may be able to comfort them which are in any trouble, by the comfort wherewith we ourselves are comforted of God" II Corr.1:3-4.

NOTES

NOTES

NOTES

ABOUT THE AUTHOR

The Author, Nathan Olubiyi is an ordained Minister of God, married to his lovely wife Izin Olubiyi. He is a father, a teacher, a musician, a composer, an administrator, and a renewable energy technologist. He also studied electrical electronics.